FROM
PREJUDICE
TO
PRIDE

A History of the LGBTQ+ Movement

BY AMY LAMÉ

WAYLAND

First published in Great Britain in 2017 by Wayland

Editor: Paul Rockett
Design: Lisa Peacock
Front cover design: Zed@They Them Studio
Picture Research: Diana Morris

ISBN: 978 1 5263 0190 1

Wayland
An imprint of
Hachette Children's Group
Part of Hodder & Stoughton
Carmelite House
50 Victoria Embankment
London EC4Y 0DZ

An Hachette UK Company
www.hachette.co.uk
www.hachettechildrens.co.uk

Printed in Singapore

Picture credits: Agateller/CC Wikimedia Commmons: 11b. alekup/Shutterstock: 33b; Robert Alexander/Archive Photos/ Getty Images: 22b; Piers Allardyce/REX/Shutterstock: 27bl; Allstar Picture Library/Alamy: 45tr; ANL/REX/Shutterstock: 52cl; Amad Badr/CC Wikimedia Commmons: 8cl; Nicholas Bailey/REX/Shutterstock: 32bl. BEI/BEI/REX/Shutterstock: 55; Bishopsgate Institute: 2t, 2cl, 2cr, 2c, 3t, 3bl, 3bc, 4, 5t, 5b, 34b, 63t, 63b, 64t, 64c, 64b; Paul Brown/REX/ Shutterstock: 20c; Mario Cabrera/AP/PAI: 31; Joel Carrett/AAP/PAI: 39c; cemT/Shutterstock: 7; Robert Clay/Alamy: 37; Massimo Consoli/CC Wikimedia Commmons: 42; Corbis/Getty Images: 25bl; Andre Csillag/REX/Shutterstock: 45tc; ddp USA/REX/Shutterstock: 28b; Clive Dixon/REX/Shutterstock: 26t; Helga Esteb/Shutterstock: 19cr, 41cl; Everett Historical/Shutterstock: 44br; Featureflash Photo Agency/Shutterstock: 41tl, 41tr; Abel Fermin/REX/Shutterstock: 50; Focus on Sport/Getty Images: 47t; Franco Folini/CC Wikimedia Commmons: 30b; David Frent/Corbis/Getty Images: 17t; Keeton Gale/Shutterstock: 41cr; David Grossmann/Alamy: 16b; Keith Hailey/Popperfoto/Getty Images: 46; David Hartley/REX/Shutterstock: 32br; Edward Hirst/REX/Shutterstock: 26br; Hulton Archive/Getty Images: 25; Images/ REX/Shutterstock: 32cl; Veera Janev/Alamy: 30c; Ozan Kose/AFP/Getty Images: 21b; lazyllama/Shutterstock: 47b; Lederhandler/AP/REX/Shutterstock: 52tr; David Lee: 21c; Lightroom Photos/Topfoto: 35cl; Steve Liss/The Life Images Collection/Getty Images: 13tr; Bill Matlock/Fox Searchlight/REX/Shutterstock: 13lc; Ben Matthews/REX/Shutterstock: 45br; Fred W McDarrah/Getty Images: 17c, 18t; Eric McGregor/Pacific Press/Lightrocket/Getty Images: 29b; Ken McKay/ITV/REX/Shutterstock: 41bl; Paul McKinnon/Shutterstock: 45bl; Ilpo Musto/REX/Shutterstock: 33ca; MY News Ltd/REX/Shutterstock: 39b; Naypong/Shutterstock: 19t; © Jeremy Nicholl. All Rights Reserved: 20b; NurPhoto/REX/ Shutterstock: 39t, 45bc; NY Daily News Archive/Getty Images: 16t; PA Extra/PA Archive/PAI: 15b; Photofusion/REX/ Shutterstock: 24t, 26bl, 28t, 48; Pictorial Press/Alamy: 45tl; REX/Shutterstock: 33c; Elzbieta Sekowska/Shutterstock: 19b; Sipa Press/REX/Shutterstock: 38, 49; Slice of Light/Flickr: 9cl; J Stone/Shutterstock: 41tr; Stonewall: 3br; Superstock: 9tl; Justin Sutcliffe/AP/PAI: 53c; Justin Tallis/AFP/Getty Images: 12; Time Life Pictures/Getty Images: 44bl; To/Variety/REX/Shutterstock: 53b; Trinity Mirror/Mirrorpix/Alamy: front cover; Tumblr: 18bl; Ullsteinbild/Getty Images: 52tl; Alan Warren/CC Wikimedia Commmons: 22cr; Wellcome Library: 25br; Reg Wilson/REX/Shutterstock: 44bc; A Life of Walt Whitman, 1905./CC Wikimedia Commmons: 22cl; Andy Wong/AP/PAI: 21t. Alex Wong/Getty Images: 36; CC Wikimedia Commmons: 8bl, 8cr, 9cr, 10, 11t, 14c, 14b, 15t, 17b, 23cl, 23cr, 23bl, 32tl, 33t, 51, 52br, 53t.

Every effort has been made to clear copyright. Should there be any inadvertent omission, please apply to the publisher for rectification.

The website addresses (URLs) included in this book were valid at the time of going to press. However, it is possible that contents or addresses may have changed since the publication of this book. No responsibility for any such changes can be accepted by either the author or the Publisher.

FOREWORD

It's important for anyone involved in a human rights movement to look back and understand what has been achieved, how it's been achieved and – crucially – who was involved.

Amy Lamé's book not only looks back at the key events in our rich history but at the diversity of people who have played a part.

It is the profiles featured in this book that to me are the most inspiring and thought-provoking.

These personal stories demonstrate that we all have the power to create change. They also underline how crucial it is for a diversity of people to be involved in the fight for equality.

If we are to achieve total acceptance of LGBT people, everyone needs to be engaged, otherwise we run the risk of creating a shallow equality, one that serves some but not others.

As this book also reflects, there are still many people living in communities where they are not able to be themselves. The fight is far from over and we can't – as individuals or as a community – forget that or become complacent.

At Stonewall we believe everyone can, and must, play a part in changing their schools, their workplaces, their places of worship and their communities so that every lesbian, gay, bi and trans person can be free to be themselves.

I hope the stories and the people celebrated in this book inspire readers to step up and realise the power they have to create a world where everyone can be accepted without exception.

Ruth Hunt,
Chief Executive of Stonewall
Stonewall is a UK-based charity that campaigns for the rights of LGBT people.

CONTENTS

ALPHABET SOUP

LGBTQ+ is a group of letters (an acronym) with each letter representing a different identity. These identities are placed together because the people who identify with them face similar issues or prejudices. Their communities often work alongside each other to fight for equal rights.

LGBTQ+ stands for:

L = lesbian

G = gay

B = bisexual

T = transgender

Q = queer or questioning

+ = includes other identities*

To be inclusive of all groups that face persecution because of their gender and sexual identity, in this book we have used the '+' sign.

You may encounter variations on this group of letters.
Here are some others that are often used:

LGBTQA

A = asexual

LGBTI

I = intersex

Sometimes these letters are all grouped together:

LGBTQIA

* For further information on identities, go to page 54.

FINDING HISTORY

LGBTQ+ history is the story of lesbian, gay, bisexual and transgender people and cultures. It includes key dates, events and organisations.

Throughout history many LGBTQ+ people have been ignored, victimised and oppressed and their voices and stories have been excluded. This can make it difficult to uncover LGBTQ+ history. Sometimes, historians have chosen to ignore or misinterpret evidence of LGBTQ+ history, telling only one side of the story. It's important to remember that all historical accounts differ depending on who is telling the story and stories often have more than one side.

We look at historical evidence to tell us what happened in the past. However, due to the secrecy, suppression and illegality of homosexuality in the past, it can sometimes be difficult to find all the historical proof needed to tell a balanced story. Sometimes we need to look in unusual places, like police records, or records of criminal court cases. In other instances, we have to 'read between the lines' to look for hidden or implied messages and meanings in order to discover LGBTQ+ history.

Now, people are becoming more aware of LGBTQ+ history. As acceptance increases, it has become an important subject and it is being woven into more conventional history. Knowing more about the past can help us understand what it means to be LGBTQ+ in the present, and what it might mean in the future.

ANCIENT CIVILISATIONS AND LGBTQ+ PEOPLE

Same-sex desire has always existed, and many ancient civilisations allowed and even encouraged its open expression. Museums around the world hold objects showing that same-sex desire has always been part of human experience.

This ancient Egyptian tomb in which two men, **Horus and Seth**, were buried together is engraved with the words '*my brother, like myself, his ways pleased me*'. It has been suggested by historians that Horus and Seth may have been a couple.

In the 18th century, European explorers recorded many examples of relationships between men in the Pacific islands. Colonial officials discouraged these relationships and forced them to continue in secret. This carved box made by the **Maori people** of New Zealand portrays images of male intimacy.

Roman emperor Hadrian (76–138 CE) built Hadrian's Wall in what was then known as Britannia, the northernmost part of the Roman Empire. He was married to a woman, but his true love was Antinous. When his lover drowned in the River Nile, Hadrian built a city in his honour – Antinopolis – near the site of his death.

The great poet **Sappho** (c. 620–570 BCE) wrote romantic poetry about love and desire for women. Only a small amount of her work survives. She lived on the Greek island of Lesbos, which is the origin of the word lesbian – to describe a woman who loves and is attracted to other women.

Someone, I say to you, will think of us in some future time.
Sappho, Fragment 147

Alexander the Great (356–323 BCE) created one of the largest empires in the ancient world, conquering lands from Greece to India. Regarded as one of the greatest military commanders who ever lived, Alexander was accompanied on his conquests by his general, bodyguard and lover Hephaestion.

Homosexuality has been documented in China for many hundreds of years. The **Han Dynasty emperor Ai** (27–1 BCE) loved his male companion Dong Xian so much that one day, after lying down for a nap, Emperor Ai cut off his sleeve rather than disturb the sleeping Dong Xian.

Some people believe we shouldn't project our modern assumptions and language about sex and gender onto the ancient world. Using words such as gay, lesbian, bisexual or transgender to refer to people in ancient history can be problematic because we don't know for sure if they thought about things in the same way that we do today. It is important to be mindful of the huge differences that not only separate us from ancient cultures but also – perhaps surprisingly – connect us.

AGAINST THE LAW!

Although some ancient cultures accepted same-sex pairings, history reveals that LGBTQ+ people have had their sexual identities and activities policed, outlawed, banned and prosecuted for centuries. Sometimes this was a result of anti-LGBTQ+ religious teachings or political beliefs which saw LGBTQ+ people as being different and therefore a threat.

Over the years, it was not uncommon for people to be imprisoned or even executed for expressing themselves. Many laws tried to control LGBTQ+ activities. However while laws can govern how people act, they cannot regulate how people feel.

Historically, the laws governing the treatment of LGBTQ+ men and women have been very different. Sexual acts between women have never been specifically outlawed in the USA and UK. Gay and bisexual men, however, have been prosecuted under laws limiting their activity.

KEY USA AND UK LAWS

1533 The **Buggery Act of England** defined anal intercourse – also known as sodomy – as 'an unnatural sexual act against the will of God and man'. Punishment was by hanging until 1861.

1885 The **Criminal Law Amendment Act** strengthened UK law against any kind of sexual activity between men under the legal term 'gross indecency'.

1962 Illinois became the first American state to remove 'consensual sodomy' from its criminal code. Prior to 1962, it was a criminal offence in every state, a law left over from when the USA was still a British colony.

1967 The **Sexual Offences Act**, UK made consensual sex between men over 21 and in private legal in England and Wales. This was extended to Scotland in 1980.

2003 The US Supreme Court removed **anti-sodomy laws** in the 14 states which still had them. However, outdated laws restricting sex between consenting adults still remain on statute books in 17 states.

Demonstrators calling for the protection of homosexuals from discrimination marched in Philadelphia, USA, 4 July, 1967.

Oscar Wilde
(1854–1900)

Oscar Wilde was an Irish author, dramatist and wit, and one of the most famous personalities of the late 19th century. He was in a tempestuous relationship with Lord Alfred, also known as 'Bosie'. Lord Alfred's father, the Marquess of Queensberry, disapproved of the relationship and publicly accused Wilde of being homosexual.

Wilde sued the Marquess for libel, but lost. When Wilde's homosexuality was confirmed by the court, he was then charged by the British government for 'gross indecency' under the Criminal Law Amendment Act. He was sentenced to two years imprisonment and hard labour.

Wilde was released from prison in 1897, fled to Paris, and changed his name. He died two years later, a man broken of body, heart and spirit. Wilde is buried in Père Lachaise Cemetery in Paris; his grave has become an important place for LGBTQ+ people to visit and pay their respects.

Oscar Wilde (left), Lord Alfred, 'Bosie' (right)

Each year, thousands of people visit Oscar Wilde's tomb (above) in Paris. A glass barrier surrounds it, covered in lipstick prints from his admirers.

HATE CRIME

Hate crime is a criminal offence motivated by prejudice towards a victim because of their real or perceived race, religion, disability, sexual orientation, ethnicity, gender or gender identity. Extreme homophobia and transphobia can sometimes lead to hate crime. LGBTQ+ people are often targeted for living outside traditional boundaries of gender and sexuality.

Hate crime can include, but is not limited to:

- verbal abuse, like name-calling
- physical attacks like hitting, punching, pushing, spitting
- bullying and harassment
- threats of violence
- hoax calls, abusive phone or text messages, hate mail
- online abuse, for example on Facebook or Twitter
- damage to things such as your home, pet, bicycle or car
- arson

Police believe hate crimes are under-reported. Victims may think the police won't support them, or they are fearful of outing themselves at home, work or school by reporting the incident.

Horrific incidents and pressure from activists have highlighted the need for courts to consider LGBTQ+ prejudice as a motivation for crime.

Transgender people are particularly vulnerable because transgender issues are still largely misunderstood and many prejudices still exist (see pages 51–53).

A vigil for hate crime victims gathers in Old Compton Street, London in 2016.

ADMIRAL DUNCAN

PEOPLE OF ALL FAITH UNITED AGAINST LGBTI HATE CRIMES

Matthew Shepard (1976–1998) was beaten, tortured, tied to a fence and left to die in Laramie, Wyoming, USA. He was discovered after 18 hours and taken to hospital but died six days later. The brutality of Shepard's death sparked outrage and led to discussions worldwide about LGBTQ+ hate crime.

Brandon Teena (1972–1993) was a trans man who was raped and murdered in Nebraska, USA. The 1999 Oscar-winning film *Boys Don't Cry* (pictured below) recounts his life and death. Teena's murder, along with that of Matthew Shepard (see above), contributed to the increased awareness of LGBTQ+ hate crime in the USA.

Actor Hilary Swank (above) played Brandon Teena in the film *Boys Don't Cry*.

A candlelight vigil for Matthew Shepard, 1998.

The **Hate Crimes Prevention Act** of 2009 was passed in the USA by President Barack Obama in honour of Matthew Shepard. It enables law enforcement officials to investigate and prosecute hate crimes.

In the UK, the **Criminal Justice Act** of 2003 requires courts to consider if a crime has been motivated by hostility to the sexual orientation (or presumed sexual orientation) of the victim and to give tougher sentences if this is true.

Jody Dobrowski (1981–2005) was a young gay man who was murdered in a homophobic attack on Clapham Common in London. The prosecution of his killers set a precedent in the UK, as it was the first time a judge applied tougher prison sentences for killers who committed an LGBTQ+ hate crime.

While reports of hate crimes are on the rise, there are still many countries around the world that do not have laws against hate crime.

13

GET POLITICAL

A number of groups fighting for equality for LGBTQ+ people began to emerge in the UK and USA in the 20th century. Many spread news of their political campaigns and protests through self-published newsletters and magazines, uniting people across their country.

USA: EARLY MOVEMENTS

The first recognised gay rights organisation in the USA was the **Society for Human Rights**, founded in Chicago in 1924 by Henry Gerber (1892–1972). The group published *Friendship and Freedom*, the first publication for homosexuals in America. Gerber and John T Graves, an African-American pastor who served as the group's president, were arrested and forced to disband the society in 1926.

A Christmas gathering of the Mattachine Society.

It took 25 years for another LGBTQ+ organisation to emerge. In 1950s' America, the 'Lavender Scare' was a period when the FBI sought out suspected LGBTQ+ people working for the government, exposed their private lives, and fired them from their jobs. LGBTQ+ people were accused of being subversive and a risk to national security during the Cold War.

This government-sanctioned harassment gave rise to the **Mattachine Society**, founded in 1950 for gay and bi men, and the **Daughters of Bilitis** founded in San Francisco in 1955 for lesbian and bi women. Their goals were tackling oppression, educating themselves and the public about homosexuality, and reducing isolation. They also aligned themselves with other civil rights movements emerging at the time, such as those fighting for racial equality and women's rights.

The Daughters of Bilitis published *The Ladder*, the first national lesbian publication in the USA. These groups were some of the very first LGBTQ+ rights groups in the world.

The October 1957 edition of The Ladder, *published by the Daughters of Bilitis.*

Phyllis Lyon (1924–present) and Del Martin (1921–2005) were the founding members of the Daughters of Bilitis (see bottom left).

UK: EARLY MOVEMENTS

In the UK the **Homosexual Law Reform Society** (HLRS) was formed in 1958 to bring together people of all sexualities who supported the Wolfenden Report (see pages 34–35). The first public meeting was held in London in May 1960; over 1,000 people attended. The group eventually achieved its goal of legalising homosexuality for men over the age of 21 in 1967.

Lesbians in the UK first organised as the **Minorities Research Group** (MRG) in 1963. This was a political and social group that provided education, support, information, and organised social events where lesbians and bi women could meet up. It also published the monthly journal *Arena Three*, Britain's first publication for lesbians and bisexual women.

The **Campaign for Homosexual Equality** (CHE) formed in 1969 and the organisation campaigned for law reform and increased access to medical and social services for LGBTQ+ people in Britain. CHE attracted a number of high profile supporters who were able to be more outspoken due to the legislation of homosexuality just two years earlier.

Little did they know, but LGBTQ+ activists at this time were about to be a part of one of the most enduring civil rights events to ever take place ...

WE'LL NOT BE TREATED AS SECOND-CLASS CITIZENS !!!

Members of the CHE attend a rally in Trafalgar Square, London, 2 November 1974.

THE STONEWALL RIOTS

The Stonewall Inn is a small LGBTQ+ bar on Christopher Street, in the Greenwich Village neighbourhood of New York City, USA. On the night of 28 June 1969, it was the site of the most important moment in LGBTQ+ history.

That night, eight police officers raided the Stonewall Inn. This wasn't unusual; LGBTQ+ people were frequently harassed, intimidated and arrested. Usually they had no choice but to surrender to the police. But this time was different; this time they fought back.

The police lined up the 200 patrons of the Stonewall Inn, checked their IDs and called for enough police vans to take all of them to jail.

Crowds formed outside the Stonewall Inn on 28 June 1969, attempting to stop police arrests.

Then, a fight started – the patrons disagreed with the way they were being treated. After being hit on the head with a baton by the police, the first punch in retaliation was thrown by Stormé DeLarverie. The patrons ran outside and other LGBTQ+ people joined them in the street. A crowd of 600 tried to overturn the police vans, then pelted them with bottles and bricks. The police barricaded themselves inside the Stonewall Inn to escape the angry, violent crowd.

By 4 a.m. things had quietened down; 14 people had been arrested, and many were injured. The next few days saw more protests, with LGBTQ+ people gathering outside the Stonewall Inn and waging heated battles with the police. Many more people were injured and arrested. But there was no turning back.

The Stonewall Inn today, Christopher Street, New York, USA

This was the birth of the modern LGBTQ+ rights movement. The brave and defiant actions of a group of lesbians, gay men and trans people fighting back against police intimidation and brutality unleashed a wave of demands for equality in the USA and beyond.

This badge from the fourth New York Pride march features a sign from the Stonewall Inn.

LEGACY

Since that night in 1969, Stonewall has come to represent the struggle for LGBTQ+ rights. Today, the Stonewall riots are commemorated in Pride celebrations around the world (see pages 18–21), and the name was adopted by the biggest LGBTQ+ rights charity in the UK.

In 2016, the Stonewall Inn was declared a National Monument, the first US National Monument commemorating the LGBTQ+ rights movement.

Members of Youth Against War & Fascism (YAWF) carry a banner at the fifth annual Pride march in New York, 30 June 1974. Here, Stonewall means resistance to oppression.

Stormé DeLarverie (1920-2014)

It was a black lesbian, Stormé DeLarverie (left), whose anger at police brutality sparked the Stonewall riots. She was a celebrated drag king and entertainer in the Jewel Box Revue, the first racially integrated drag show in the USA. She went on to become an outspoken advocate for the LGBTQ+ community and victims of domestic abuse. Stormé later became known as the 'Lesbian Guardian of Greenwich Village', for her voluntary street patrol work. A film about her life, *Stormé: The Lady of the Jewel Box*, was released in 1987.

WHAT IS PRIDE?

The term 'Pride' refers to a public statement in defence of the rights of LGBTQ+ people. In many LGBTQ+ communities, Pride events include marches, parades and festivals. These are usually held on days which are significant to the community, such as important anniversaries.

The first Pride march was held in New York City in June 1970 (pictured right) to commemorate the one-year anniversary of the Stonewall riots. It was originally called the Christopher Street Liberation Day March, after the street where the Stonewall Inn is located.

Other communities around the world soon began organising their own versions of the march. As they became more widely popular in the 1980s, the marches became known as Gay Pride. Now the terms LGBT Pride or Pride are also widely used. Many marches still have a political element as well as celebrating LGBTQ+ life, love and culture.

Pride is an important event because it reminds people of the Stonewall riots, a crucial moment in the struggle for LGBTQ+ rights and equality. Pride is a time to come together, show strength, and share stories with those who have been through similar struggles. Pride makes the LGBTQ+ community more visible, vocal and powerful.

Brenda Howard (1946–2005), pictured below, left, is known as the **'Mother of Pride'.** She was a bisexual activist and organised the first Pride march. She came up with the idea for an annual LGBTQ+ festival.

The worldwide symbol of LGBTQ+ Pride is the rainbow flag. It was designed in 1978 by Gilbert Baker (1951–present) after he was asked by Harvey Milk (see page 37) to create a symbol of gay pride. The colours represent the diversity of the LGBTQ+ community. It is flown or hung with the red stripe at the top. Wherever the rainbow flag is flown across the globe, LGBTQ+ people are especially welcome.

In 2016, New York hosted one of the biggest Pride celebrations, with around 32,000 marchers.

> ❝ You should be proud of being different. You should be proud of who you are. ❞
> *Ellen DeGeneres, American comedian*

PRIDE AROUND THE WORLD

Pride events take place annually in thousands of towns and cities across the world. As LGBTQ+ equality grows, so do the number of Pride celebrations. However, in some countries, Pride is banned, and in others it is still not safe for LGBTQ+ people to take part in the event.

RUSSIA

Pride marches began in Moscow in 2006. In June 2012, all LGBTQ+ Pride parades were banned by the government for the next 100 years. There is no law in Russia to stop discrimination against LGBTQ+ people.

UK

In 1970, 700 gay men marched for equality on Highbury Fields in London; this was the beginning of Pride in the UK. In 2016, 750,000 people attended, and 30,000 lined the streets of London to cheer them on. Pride events happen in towns and cities across the UK including Belfast, Brighton, Birmingham, Cardiff and Glasgow.

CHINA

Shanghai was the first Chinese city to host a Pride event in 2009. Chinese laws make it illegal to organise marches, though Guangzhou and Chengdu have launched Pride events in recent years.

SOUTH AFRICA

The first Pride event to take place on the African continent was in Johannesburg, South Africa, in 1990. South Africa's post-apartheid constitution made it the first country in the world to explicitly prohibit discrimination based on sexual orientation, but homophobia is still a problem in many communities.

TURKEY

Istanbul has held Pride marches since 2003. It started with just 30 people, growing to 100,000 in 2013, making it one of the largest Pride events in the Middle East. However, at Istanbul Pride in 2015 police attacked the crowd with water cannons, and 2016 Pride was banned by the city government.

PRE-LIBERATION PIONEERS

Some brave LGBTQ+ people lived their lives openly before liberation, even though it was dangerous, socially unacceptable and even illegal to live honestly. Their fearlessness helped pave the way for future generations of out and proud LGBTQ+ people.

Writing is one way pioneers expressed themselves. They were able to reach out to a wide audience and give hope to other LGBTQ+ people.

Walt Whitman

The father of modern American literature, **Walt Whitman** (1819–1892), wrote his iconic collection of poems, *Leaves of Grass*, in 1855. It boldly celebrates sexuality and caused outrage when it was published.

Whitman's brave writing influenced the writer and social critic **James Baldwin** (1924–1987). Baldwin experienced intense prejudice for being black and gay in America, and wove the issues of racism and homophobia into his writing. His groundbreaking 1956 novel, *Giovanni's Room*, depicts homosexuality and bisexuality with honesty and compassion.

James Baldwin

Another fearless author, the civil rights activist **Audre Lorde** (1934–1992), wrote *Zami: A New Spelling of My Name*. It tells a story of black lesbian identity through autobiography and mythology. A number of LGBTQ+ organisations are named in Lorde's honour.

Audre Lorde

Popular entertainment allowed some courageous LGBTQ+ people to express themselves on stage. Dressing up played an important part in this.

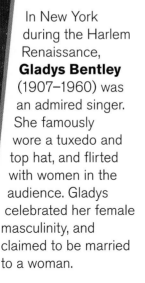
Fanny & Stella

Fanny and Stella were the stage names of **Frederick William Park** (1848–1881) and **Thomas Ernest Boulton** (1848–1904), a British cross-dressing theatrical duo. Traditionally, cross-dressing was allowed on stage but not in public. They were arrested for wearing dresses in the streets of London and for suspected homosexuality.

In New York during the Harlem Renaissance, **Gladys Bentley** (1907–1960) was an admired singer. She famously wore a tuxedo and top hat, and flirted with women in the audience. Gladys celebrated her female masculinity, and claimed to be married to a woman.

Gladys Bentley

Women faced many hurdles to overcome both sexism and homophobia in society.

Anne Lister

The British mountaineer, diarist, and traveller **Anne Lister** (1791–1840) wrote about her relationships with women. Lister lived her life openly and was accepted by her local community; she is thought of as the first modern lesbian.

The American heroine **Jane Addams** (1860–1935) was a progressive social activist and author, and was awarded the Nobel Peace Prize in 1931. With her partner Ellen Starr, she founded Hull House in Chicago, which provided education for impoverished women. Addams lived in a 'Boston marriage' – a term used to describe two women living independently of men – with Mary Rozett Smith for 40 years.

Jane Addams

EARLY SOCIAL AND POLITICAL GROUPS

Demonstrators take part in a LGBTQ+ rights protest march in London, 198

The LGBTQ+ community is a local, national and global group of people who come from all backgrounds, races, beliefs and genders, and who share some things about their sexual identity.

It is estimated that between 5 to 10 per cent of the world's population is LGBTQ+. That's a lot of people!

Being part of a community can be empowering; it allows us to share experiences, form friendships and work towards common goals. Community shows us we are part of humanity, and that we are all connected in some way.

FINDING EACH OTHER

Throughout most periods in history, it could be difficult for LGBTQ+ people to identify each other. Dedicated social spaces were rare and the threat of arrest and imprisonment was never far away. But LGBTQ+ people are resourceful, and they have always found ways to communicate and signal their identity to others like them.

In late 19th century Britain some men – including Oscar Wilde – wore a green carnation as a symbol of their sexuality. In the 20th century the use of *polari* – a form of slang – enabled gay men to speak to each other in a coded language only they could understand. In the 1960s, several gay comedians played characters who used polari in popular television and radio shows. This allowed them to signal their identity to others, while also allowing them to hide in plain sight.

From the 1950s onwards lesbians sometimes wore a pinky ring (a ring on the little finger) as a signifier. This was a sign, dating back to Victorian times (1837–1901), to indicate that you were uninterested in marriage.

SPEAK POLARI!

bona – good

vada – to see

dolly – pretty, nice

eek – face

riah – hair

omi – man

palone – woman

zshooshy – fancy, showy

TURNING IT AROUND

The pink triangle was used by the Nazis during the Second World War (1939–1945) to identify gay men who were imprisoned in concentration camps in Europe. In the 1980s, LGBTQ+ activists took this symbol of shame and victimisation, and used it as a symbol of defiance, liberation and dignity.

Gay prisoners at the concentration camp at Sachsenhausen, Germany, wearing pink triangles on their uniforms, 19 December 1938.

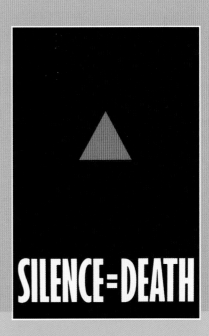

SILENCE=DEATH

The group AIDS Coalition To Unleash Power (ACT UP) turned the pink triangle the other way round and used it as part of its slogan that encouraged the LGBTQ+ community to speak out for action in fighting AIDS (see pages 31–33).

A GROWING MOVEMENT

After the Stonewall riots in 1969, groups like the Mattachine Society and the Daughters of Bilitis could be more open and many more community groups formed. Some had a strong political element, like the **Gay Liberation Front** (GLF), which began in New York and had branches around the world. The London group started in 1970 and was particularly active, staging protests like drag kiss-ins. By 1974 the GLF had disbanded, but other community groups were created.

A Gay Liberation Front demonstration in the UK, 1971.

Many, like the **London Lesbian and Gay Switchboard**, a free helpline, and the weekly UK publication *Gay News*, became important community resources. Direct action groups like the **Lesbian Avengers** in the USA were founded to increase awareness of issues facing lesbians, while **OutRage!** in the UK was established to protest against homophobia. Activist Peter Tatchell (1952–present) was a founding member of OutRage! and is a vocal campaigner for LGBTQ+ rights around the world.

Angela Mason (1944–present) was also a member of the GLF; she went on to lead **Stonewall**, a UK charity that fights for LGBTQ+ rights. It works with organisations to bring equality to LGBTQ+ people at home, at school and at work.

Angela Mason

Actor Sir Ian McKellen (1939–present) is a co-founder of Stonewall, the largest LGBTQ+ rights organisation in Europe.

SOCIAL SPACES AND NIGHTLIFE

A safe space is a place where anyone can relax and express themselves without fear of discrimination. Safe social spaces, such as cafés, nightclubs, bars and members clubs, are very important to LGBTQ+ people; everyone deserves the opportunity to enjoy themselves and relax with friends.

MOLLY HOUSES

The idea of an organised LGBTQ+ meeting place started in 18th and 19th century England, when homosexual men could meet and socialise in a molly-house. These were taverns or coffee houses, but they were not so safe; molly-houses were often raided by police.

HISTORIC SPACES

London's Royal Vauxhall Tavern (below) is one of the oldest LGBTQ+ social spaces in the UK; the pub has attracted gay customers since the 1940s. It is still a thriving space for the LGBTQ+ community. In 2015 the building was listed and given protection by Historic England for its importance to LGBTQ+ history – the first ever in the UK.

LGBTQ+ FRIENDLY

Many social spaces, like restaurants, cafés and shops, signal that they are safe and LGBTQ+ friendly spaces by putting a rainbow sticker in the window.

Mourners outside the Admiral Duncan pub, London, 1999.

HOW SAFE IS SAFE?

Places that are havens for LGBTQ+ people are still at risk of attack.

In 1999, the Admiral Duncan pub in Soho, an area in London that has been popular with the LGBTQ+ community for many years, was bombed in a homophobic attack. Three people were killed and 70 were injured.

On 12 June 2016, the Pulse nightclub in Orlando, Florida was attacked; 49 people were killed and 53 were injured. It was the deadliest incident of violence against LGBTQ+ people in US history.

Despite wider acceptance of LGBTQ+ people, in the face of discrimination and threats of violence, safe spaces are still important for the LGBTQ+ community.

A temporary memorial formed outside the Pulse nightclub, Orlando, USA, after the attack.

COMMUNITY IN ACTION

As laws change and become more inclusive, LGBTQ+ people are more comfortable being open about their identity. Community groups offer support, camaraderie and connection. There are LGBTQ+ focused groups for just about every kind of interest!

CenterLink is a network of LGBTQ+ community centres across the USA. There were only two community centres in 1971; now, there are over 250 from Portland, Oregon to Hattiesburg, Mississippi and hundreds of towns and cities in between. CenterLink helps support thriving community centres that advance the safety, equality and well being of LGBTQ+ people.

Gendered Intelligence works in the UK trans community to support diverse gender expressions, especially with young people. **School's Out** was originally the Gay Teachers Association, founded in 1974. It strives to make all UK schools safe spaces for LGBTQ+ students, teachers, parents and staff.

The **Audre Lorde Project** – named after the lesbian writer – is a community centre in New York City for LGBTQ+ people of colour. Its advocacy and activities support people facing multiple layers of discrimination.

The 12th annual Trans Day of Action in New York City (right), organised by the Audre Lorde Project to raise awareness of social and economic justice for the trans community.

Bookshops play an important part in LGBTQ+ community building. They sell books, distribute newsletters, host events and offer spaces where community news can be shared.

In London, **Gay's The Word** bookshop (below), founded in 1979, hosted the important Lesbians and Gays Support the Miners group (LGSM), that raised money and campaigned with coal miners striking in the 1980s. Their story was retold in the 2014 film *Pride*.

In Liverpool, **News from Nowhere** is still a hub for LGBTQ+ readers. In Philadelphia, **Giovanni's Room**, founded in 1973 is the oldest LGBTQ+ bookshop in the USA. It's named after a book by James Baldwin (see page 22).

> ❝ Gay's the Word is not just a bookshop, but the hub and affirmation of a whole community. ❞
> Sarah Waters, author

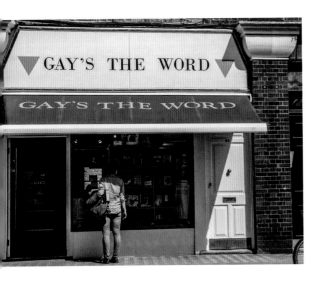

SOCIAL GROUPS

Many LGBTQ+ people find a community in social groups such as choirs and social sports teams.

The **LGBTQ+ choral movement** is a collection of over 250 choirs around the world. The first and largest is the **San Francisco Gay Men's Chorus** (below) which was founded in 1978 and has over 300 members.

The first openly gay rugby team in the world, the **King's Cross Steelers**, was founded in London in 1995. The **Gay Games** is the world's largest sporting event specifically for LGBTQ+ athletes. It is held in a different city every four years, and in 2018 will be held in Paris.

HIV, or Human Immunodeficiency Virus, causes AIDS (Acquired Immune Deficiency Syndrome), which is the most advanced stage of HIV infection. HIV wears down the body's immune system, making most people who have the virus very vulnerable to serious infections.

While there is no cure, many people who are HIV-positive take powerful and effective medication and live completely normal lives. However, this medication has not always been available, and when HIV first became widespread, doctors and governments were unprepared to manage the large numbers of people who were infected.

HIV and AIDS can affect anyone, though some groups of people are at higher risk than others. The virus may be transmitted through sexual contact, from semen, vaginal and cervical secretions, and can also be found in blood, amniotic fluid and breast milk. In the UK and US, when HIV and AIDS first emerged, gay and bisexual men were the community most affected by the disease.

In the early 1980s, many gay and bisexual men began to show signs of unusual infections. At the time, nobody knew what HIV was, and the illness did not even have a name.

The illness spread very quickly, and devastated LGBTQ+ communities. Prejudice and homophobia also meant that many LGBTQ+ people who had AIDS were discriminated against because they were ill. While it was clear that the disease had not originated from gay men or just infected gay men, many in the mainstream media labelled AIDS as the 'gay plague' despite the facts. This increased homophobia, as well as fear and anxiety for the gay community.

LGBTQ+ activist groups, such as ACT UP (above), were very important in fighting for increased awareness and research into HIV and AIDS and ways to treat it.

Since the beginning of the epidemic about 35 million people have died of HIV, with over 36 million people living with HIV at the end of 2015.

Now, most people who are HIV-positive do not progress to having AIDS. Prescribed medication can keep the level of HIV low, reduce the likelihood of AIDS, and lower the risk of transmitting HIV to others. Using condoms during sex is the most effective way to prevent infection.

HIV & AIDS TIMELINE

Terrence Higgins

Rock Hudson

AIDS
DON'T DIE
OF
IGNORANCE

1981	270 reported cases of gay men with AIDS in the USA; 121 die.
1982	**Gay Men's Health Crisis** (GMHC) founded in New York, USA. **Terrence Higgins** dies – one of the first British men to die from the disease. The **Terrence Higgins Trust**, the UK's first HIV and AIDS organisation, was set up in his memory.
1985	Testing for HIV begins in the UK. American actor **Rock Hudson** dies of AIDS-related illness, age 59. He is the first major public figure to acknowledge that he has AIDS, and leaves $250,000 to help set up the **American Foundation for AIDS Research**.
1986	HIV (human immunodeficiency virus) is adopted as the name of the virus which causes AIDS.
1987	AIDS activist Cleve Jones creates the first panel of the **AIDS Memorial Quilt**, a hand-stitched quilt with each panel representing the life of someone who died from AIDS. Playwright and AIDS activist **Larry Kramer** founds the campaign and direct action group **ACT UP** (the AIDS Coalition to Unleash Power) in New York City. The UK government's 'Don't Die of Ignorance' campaign is launched, with leaflets delivered to every home in the country. Princess Diana shakes hands and poses for photos with a man dying from AIDS. There was a popular belief that touching AIDS patients could spread the disease. She was important in challenging this false information.

"HIV does not make people dangerous to know, so you can shake their hands and give them a hug. Heaven knows they need it."

Princess Diana (1961–1997), mother of Prince William and Harry

1988 1 December is designated **World AIDS Day**.

The gay African-American entertainer **Sylvester** dies of AIDS-related illness, age 41.

1990 American pop artist and AIDS activist **Keith Haring** dies of AIDS-related illness, age 31.

1991 The red ribbon becomes the international symbol of AIDS awareness.

Freddie Mercury, British lead singer/songwriter of the rock band Queen, dies of AIDS-related illness, age 45.

World-renowned Russian ballet dancer **Rudolf Nureyev** dies of AIDS-related illness, age 54.

The film *Philadelphia*, starring Tom Hanks as a lawyer fired from his job because he has AIDS, opens in cinemas. Hanks won an Academy Award for his role. This film was the first time mainstream media had addressed HIV and AIDS.

1994 In this year, AIDS becomes the leading cause of death for all Americans between the ages of 25 and 44.

1995 Combination therapy – a mix of therapeutic medicines – is introduced for HIV-positive people; it proves effective in slowing the virus and prolonging lives.

2008 The Nobel Prize in medicine is awarded to two French virologists, **Françoise Barré-Sinoussi** and **Luc A Montagnier**, for their 1983 discovery of HIV, the virus that causes AIDS.

2009 President Barack Obama launches the first National HIV/AIDS Strategy for the United States. He also lifts the travel ban that prevents HIV-positive people from entering the US.

2016 The UK government approves **PrEP** for HIV, a medication for people at very high risk of contracting HIV to lower their chances of getting infected.

The US Centers for Disease Control and Prevention reports that only 1 in 5 sexually active high school students has been tested for HIV. An estimated 50 per cent of young Americans who are living with HIV do not know they are infected.

Sylvester

Freddie Mercury

Rudolf Nureyev

DECRIMINALISATION

In the early 1950s several well-known men in Britain, including the actor Sir John Gielgud and code breaker Alan Turing, were arrested and convicted of homosexual offences. The prosecution of these respected public figures led to an examination of the law.

THE WOLFENDEN REPORT

In 1954 the British government asked Sir John Wolfenden to form the Wolfenden Committee. It was a group of lawyers, researchers, politicians, doctors and religious leaders whose job was to explore the possibility of making homosexuality legal in the UK.

After conducting research, including interviews with gay men, the Wolfenden Report was presented to the government in 1957. It recommended that homosexual behaviour between consenting adults in private should no longer be a crime.

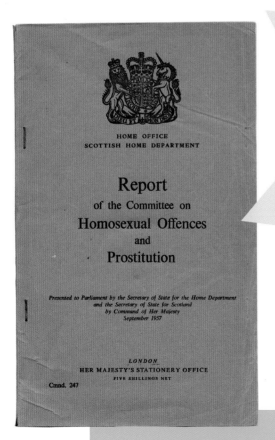

> **"It is not, in our view, the function of the law to intervene in the private life of citizens, or to seek to enforce any particular pattern of behaviour."**
> *Wolfenden Report*

HOME OFFICE
SCOTTISH HOME DEPARTMENT

Report
of the Committee on
Homosexual Offences
and
Prostitution

Presented to Parliament by the Secretary of State for the Home Department
and the Secretary of State for Scotland
by Command of Her Majesty
September 1957

LONDON
HER MAJESTY'S STATIONERY OFFICE
FIVE SHILLINGS NET

Cmnd. 247

There was a lot of public debate and it took ten years for the law to be changed. Finally, the Sexual Offences Act 1967 made homosexuality legal for adult men aged 21 and over in England and Wales.

Cover of the Wolfenden Report, 1957.

Alan Turing (1912–1954)

The death of Alan Turing was a tragic moment in Britain's history. Turing was a national hero. He developed a machine (the Bombe) capable of cracking encrypted Enigma messages during the Second World War, playing a crucial role in the Allies defeating the Nazis and winning the war. It is estimated that his groundbreaking work shortened the war by four years, saving millions of lives. After the war he worked in a laboratory and invented some of the first known computers.

In 1952, five years before the Wolfenden Report, Turing was prosecuted for 'gross indecency' – as homosexual offences were then called – and fired from his job. In order to avoid going to prison Turing accepted experimental chemical castration as punishment. He committed suicide in 1954, aged 42. Many believe he killed himself because of the pain and shame involved in his sexual identity and public punishment.

Turing is now recognised as the father of computer science and artificial intelligence. In 2009, 55 years after his death, the UK government apologised, calling Turing's treatment 'horrifying' and 'utterly unfair'.

The Sexual Offences Act legalised homosexuality in England and Wales. Here are some dates when it was decriminalised around the world.

 FRANCE – 1791

 ARGENTINA – 1887

 DENMARK – 1933

 CANADA – 1969

 SPAIN – 1979

 SCOTLAND – 1980

 AUSTRALIA – 1989

 IRELAND – 1993

 USA – 2003

TOWARDS EQUALITY

Changing the law is often the first step in changing people's attitudes. LGBTQ+ groups have worked hard with governments and political parties to increase equality in all areas of life. One important way to do this was to fight against rules and traditions which kept LGBTQ+ people invisible in areas such as politics and the armed forces.

'DON'T ASK, DON'T TELL'

Until 1993, LGBT people were all banned from serving in the US armed forces. In 1993 the 'Don't Ask, Don't Tell' policy was introduced. This meant that LGB people would be allowed to serve, but under special rules: the armed forces couldn't directly ask serving members about their sexual orientation. It also meant that LGB people in the armed forces could be dismissed for openly talking about their sexuality, marrying someone of the same sex, or even having a relationship with somebody of the same sex. In 2010, the US government signed a law abolishing 'Don't Ask, Don't Tell'. The ban on transgender people serving in the US armed forces was lifted in 2016.

In the UK, campaigning by LGBTQ+ rights groups such as Stonewall, led to the lifting of the ban on lesbians, gay men and bisexual people serving in the armed forces in 2000.

A US Army veteran is arrested close to members of the civil rights organisation GetEqual. They handcuffed themselves to the fence outside the White House, Washington DC, in protest against 'Don't Ask, Don't Tell' in November 2010.

Between 1997 and 2010 the UK government did more for the advancement of LGBTQ+ equality than any other government in global history, including:

- Introduced an equal age of consent for all, regardless of gender or sexuality.

- Granted equal rights to same-sex couples who want to adopt children, and recognised same-sex partners for immigration purposes.

- Created the Gender Recognition Act, allowing trans people to have their true gender recognised in law.

- Introduced civil partnerships, allowing LGB people to have their relationships recognised by law and the same benefits as married couples.

Harvey Milk (1930-1978)

Harvey Milk was the first openly gay man elected to office in San Francisco, in the USA. He was voted onto the City Board of Supervisors in 1977.

A champion of equality, he was a charismatic leader, and worked to pass groundbreaking city legislation banning discrimination based on sexual orientation.

Harvey Milk's high profile as an out gay politician made him a target for homophobic violence, and on 27 November 1978, he was murdered by a fellow city supervisor. The Mayor of San Francisco, Mayor Moscone, was also killed in the attack.

> **"**If a bullet should enter my brain, let that bullet destroy every closet door.**"**
>
> *Harvey Milk*

Many books have been written about Harvey Milk, and in 2008 an Oscar-winning film about him, *Milk*, was released. He was awarded the Presidential Medal of Freedom posthumously in 2009, and 22 May is designated as Harvey Milk Day. Several cities have named streets after him, and the Harvey Milk Foundation is a charity which works to keep his trailblazing legacy alive.

EQUAL MARRIAGE

Marriage is the legal union of two people in either a civil (non-religious) or a religious ceremony. Not all countries allow equal marriage, also known as same-sex or gay marriage. Those countries which do allow it have only recently made it possible.

Marriage is regarded as a significant commitment and an important family bond. It also gives both partners particular legal rights, benefits and obligations, such as the right to inheritance if one partner were to die.

The Netherlands was the first country in the world to introduce equal marriage, in 2001. Now 20 nations around the world have equal marriage laws, including South Africa (2006), Mexico (2010), England and Wales (2013), Scotland (2014) and the USA (all states by 2015).

Major Michael Bloomberg oversees the first day when same-sex marriages could take place in New York, USA, on 24 July 2011.

DIFFERENT FAITHS

Historically most marriages have taken place in a religious context. Different religious communities have different attitudes towards LGBTQ+ people, and this means that many religions have had to consider the question of equal marriage. While the law of a country might make equal marriage legal, religious leaders cannot be forced to carry out marriage ceremonies for people of the same sex.

I DO/I DON'T

Equal marriage has caused much controversy. Some people believe marriage should only be between a man and a woman. Not all LGBTQ+ people believe equal marriage is a good thing, either. Some see marriage as an outmoded institution and argue that imitating 'straight' relationships fosters a 'heteronormative' outlook – promoting heterosexuality as the normal or preferred way of living.

The fight for equal marriage has been a hugely important one for LGBTQ+ people and supportive allies. This is because the right to marry is one of the most visible civil rights people can have.

Women marry on the first day that same-sex marriage became legal in New Jersey, USA, on 21 October 2013.

FIGHT FOR THE RIGHT TO MARRY

In 2008, voters in California voted for Proposition 8, which changed the marriage laws in the state, and defined marriage as only between a man and a woman. After a fierce battle, the Supreme Court ruled in 2013 that same-sex marriages could be performed in California. This success paved the way for other states to pass similar legislation. In 2015, same-sex marriage became legal nationwide in the USA.

There are many LGBTQ+ people still fighting for same-sex marriage in other countries around the world, such as Australia (see above picture).

The UK introduced civil partnerships in 2004, allowing same-sex couples to obtain essentially the same rights and responsibilities as civil marriage. Equal marriage – opening the possibility of the union taking place in a house of worship – came into force in 2014, though not in Northern Ireland.

These men were one of the first gay couples to get married in Britain, on 28 March 2014.

COMING OUT

The act of an LBGTQ+ person accepting their sexuality or gender identity is known as 'coming out'. The metaphor 'coming out of the closet' is also used, meaning the person no longer wants to hide their true self away.

For some LGBTQ+ people, coming out involves telling something about themselves which isn't immediately obvious to those around them. For others it means living their identity publicly, without having to hide aspects of themselves. It can be the most important and challenging moment in many LGBTQ+ people's lives. Admitting your true identity requires courage and strength and can feel confusing or scary, but hiding who you are can also be a big struggle and be very distracting. Coming out is different for everyone.

TALKING TO YOUR FAMILY

Often the most difficult people to come out to, besides oneself, are parents or guardians. It can be difficult to predict what may happen, or how they may react. Some young people may lose the support of their parents and even be forced to leave the family home. Others find it easier, and develop closer relationships with their families.

It may take time for some families to understand and accept LGBTQ+ family members, while others may accept them more quickly. Every situation, like every family, is different.

OUTING

Not everyone chooses to come out. Some people keep their true identity secret because of fear, family pressure or religion. Others aren't quite ready to come out yet. No one should be forced to come out before they are ready. Use of social media and the Internet means that news spreads much faster these days than it used to.

Some people have been forced to come out before they are ready, or without their consent. This is often called 'outing'. It is sometimes used as a way of shaming, or degrading, LGBTQ+ people in public, and is a violation of their right to privacy.

OUR HISTORIES

Sharing 'coming out stories' is a vital part of LGBTQ+ life, recognising the joys and struggles of living openly and honestly. Our personal stories connect us with the past and help us look towards the future. The importance of LGBTQ+ history is illuminated with each and every coming out story, reminding us that we are part of a greater community, and reflecting on the struggles of those who came before.

"I hadn't been happy in so long. I've been sad again since, but it's a totally different take on sad. There's just some magic in truth and honesty and openness."

Frank Ocean, American singer/songwriter

"I'm proud to be gay, and I consider being gay among the greatest gifts God has given me."

Tim Cook, American Businessman
and CEO of Apple Inc.

"There was a time when all of us were closeted and we remember what a scary, awful place that is ... my coming out process was the way it was, it wasn't perfect by any means, but I sure learned a lot from it."

Chaz Bono, American actor and activist

"My dad and my mom have always told me, 'Be who you are'. At the time, they probably weren't sure what I was interpreting that as."

Brittney Griner, Women's National Basketball
Association player for US team Phoenix Mercury

"I got to the point where I couldn't sleep, I couldn't blink, I was afraid of the dark all of a sudden. So I needed to find the strength to tell the truth to people."

Gareth Thomas, former captain of the
Welsh Rugby Team and first out rugby player

"I am tired of hiding and I am tired of lying by omission ... I suffered for years because I was scared to be out. I'm here today because I am gay."

Ellen Page, Canadian actor

MEDIA

LGBTQ+ representation in mainstream media has largely been full of stereotypes – an oversimplified, incorrect and sometimes offensive idea of who LGBTQ+ people are and how they think and behave.

FILMS

Any open portrayal of LGBTQ+ lives in films was prohibited in Hollywood from 1930 to 1968, under Article 4 of The Motion Picture Production Code. It banned 'any inference of sex perversion' which was understood to mean homosexuality. The LGBTQ+ movement fought back and campaigned for more visibility and realistic portrayals of LGBTQ+ characters. One way they did that was to organise LGBTQ+ film festivals, which showed films and documentaries made for and by LGBTQ+ people. Today, these festivals take place in cities all over the globe. The San Francisco International LGBTQ Film Festival, which was founded in 1977, is the longest running one in the world.

Vito Russo (1946–1990)

Russo was an American activist, writer and film historian. His 1981 book, *The Celluloid Closet*, uncovered contributions LGBTQ+ people made to the world of cinema.

He was so distressed by the way LGBTQ+ and HIV-positive people were represented in the media, he co-founded the **Gay and Lesbian Alliance Against Defamation** (GLAAD), a media watchdog group.

GLAAD monitors how LGBTQ+ people are represented in the media, and works with print, broadcast and online news to bring LGBTQ+ stories into the mainstream.

Russo died, aged 44, from AIDS-related illness. In 2013, GLAAD named the 'Vito Russo test' after him, a set of criteria to analyse LGBTQ+ characters and representation in films.

PRINT AND ONLINE

LGBTQ+ focused media is hugely important in informing and connecting people. Traditionally these were photocopied newsletters or printed magazines and newspapers. With availability of the Internet from 1990, LGBTQ+ media became huge, including blogs, online news sites, YouTube channels and more.

Social media plays an important role in LGBTQ+ life; hashtags on Twitter such as *#LoveisLove* and *#ItGetsBetter* make it possible to access positive, affirming messages, especially in the face of online homophobia.

TELEVISION

LGBTQ+ people are more visible on television and streaming entertainment than they have ever been. However, according to GLAAD, only 4.8 per cent of all characters on mainstream TV or streaming shows are identified at LGBTQ+. They also found that very few shows represent HIV-positive characters. More visibility and better representations are still a challenge that LGBTQ+ activists are fighting for.

LGBTQ+ LANDMARKS IN ENTERTAINMENT MEDIA

1971 First gay character in a US sitcom – on *All in the Family*, a working class comedy.

1972 *That Certain Summer*, a US made-for-TV film, is the first to deal sympathetically with male homosexuality.

The BBC air the drama *Girl*, which features the first lesbian kiss on UK TV.

1975 First sympathetic representation of a trans character in a TV series appears on *The Jeffersons*, a popular US sitcom about an African-American family.

1986 The first gay male kiss on UK TV happens – on soap opera *EastEnders*.

1991 First homosexual kiss on US TV – between a female couple on *L.A. Law*.

1994 Ikea is the first store to run a TV advertisement featuring a gay couple.

1998 The first permanent trans character in a drama series appears in the UK's soap opera *Coronation Street*.

1999 Groundbreaking British TV series *Queer as Folk* follows three gay men and their lives in the gay village area of Manchester. It becomes a US series in 2000, set in Pittsburgh.

2005 *Brokeback Mountain*, a Hollywood film about two gay cowboys starring Heath Ledger and Jake Gyllenhaal, is released; it goes on to win three Oscars.

2012 The D.C. Comic character Green Lantern, who first appeared in 1940, is revealed as a gay man.

2015 *I Am Cait* airs, the docudrama/reality show about Caitlyn Jenner's transition.

MUSIC

Music – especially by LGBTQ+ artists – plays a powerful role in helping LGBTQ+ people feel connected and less alone. Until recently, coming out for musicians, composers, and singers was often seen as an end to their career. Nowadays, some find it easier to come out professionally, and if they do, some even see a boost in their popularity. When celebrities and public figures open up about who they are, their visibility can be especially useful in fighting prejudice and homophobia.

Influential LGBTQ+ composers and musicians:

Pyotr Tchaikovsky (1840–1893), Russian composer of *The Nutcracker* and *Swan Lake*

Benjamin Britten (1913–1976), British conductor and composer who wrote many songs for his lover, Peter Pears.

Billy Tipton (1914–1989) a popular American bandleader and musician who was biologically female but lived life as a man, a fact only discovered after he had died.

Bessie Smith (1894–1937), one of the most popular singers of the 1920s and 30s was known as the 'Empress of the Blues' and had both male and female partners.

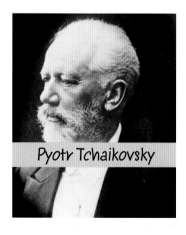

Pyotr Tchaikovsky

Benjamin Britten

Bessie Smith

Divine

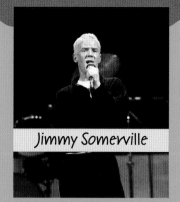

Jimmy Somerville

George Michael

Disco was the post-liberation soundtrack after the Stonewall riots. Openly trans/gay artists like **Sylvester** (1947–1988) and **Divine** (1945–1988) were popular performers and sang out and proud lyrics that appealed to LGBTQ+ audiences.

The first out rock star was **Jobriath** (1946–1983), an unapologetically gay American artist. Soon after his first album was released in 1972 Jobriath vanished from the public eye, and died from an AIDS-related illness aged 36.

Bisexual British artist **Tom Robinson**'s (1950–) 1976 anthem 'Sing If You're Glad To Be Gay' broke barriers for confronting homophobic attitudes in the UK, as did **Bronski Beat**'s 1984 worldwide hit 'Smalltown Boy'. It tells a stark tale of a young gay man who is homophobically attacked and leaves home to seek acceptance in the big city. It was written and sung by out Scottish gay pop star **Jimmy Somerville** (1961–).

George Michael (1963–2016) was one of the most successful British pop stars ever. He was outed as gay in the USA in 1998. This did not affect his popularity, and he continued to sell millions of albums worldwide.

Canadian country artist and multiple Grammy Award winner **k.d. lang** (1961–) came out in 1992; her androgynous look was a first for successful women in the music industry.

Mercury Music Prize winner and Oscar nominated British singer songwriter **Anohni** (1971–) became well known as the lead singer of indie band **Antony and the Johnsons**. Formally known as Antony Hegarty, she came out as trans in 2016.

Trailblazing French singer songwriter **Heloise Letissier** (1988–), aka **Christine and the Queens**, identifies as pansexual and found inspiration for her music and shows from London's drag queens.

k.d. lang

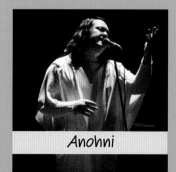

Anohni

Christine and the Queens

SPORT

Some see sport as the 'last frontier' for LGBTQ+ people – a realm where it can be extremely difficult to come out, at an amateur or professional level.

Gender stereotypes, bullying and a lack of visible LGBTQ+ sports people make many LGBTQ+ athletes feel that sports or sports teams might not welcome them. However, sports should be everyone's game, and a few trailblazers have helped to pave the way, although some of their stories have had heartbreaking consequences. This is partly due to homophobia among players and supporters – and a lack of awareness of the issues faced by LGBTQ+ people.

Justin Fashanu (1961–1998)

To date, there are no openly gay or bi male football players in the top divisions of UK football. Justin Fashanu was the first professional British football star to come out as gay. He was also Britain's first black football player to sign a £1 million contract. While playing for Nottingham Forest FC, the coach wouldn't allow Fashanu to train with his teammates because of his sexuality. Fashanu came out publicly in a newspaper interview in 1990, and suffered homophobic taunts from his teammates, football fans and the press. After he came out, no team would offer him a full-time contract.

In May 1998 he committed suicide; it is believed Fashanu's harsh treatment as a black gay football player contributed to his death. The Justin Campaign has been set up in his honour to combat homophobia in football. LGBTQ+ football fans have set up an online campaign, *#PrideinFootball*, and the Rainbow Laces campaign urges athletes to wear rainbow laces to help raise awareness of homophobia in sport.

Billie Jean King
(1943-)

Winner of a record 20 Wimbledon titles and founder of the Women's Tennis Association, in 1981 American Billie Jean King was the first athlete to come out as lesbian. In fact, King was outed against her wishes when a lawsuit, filed by her former partner, was made public. King lost all her professional endorsements, worth $2 million, and was subjected to public humiliation in the press. She now campaigns to end homophobia in sport.

> **I couldn't get a closet deep enough. I've got a homophobic family, a tour that will die if I come out, the world is homophobic and, yeah, I was homophobic. If you speak with gays, bisexuals, lesbians and transgenders, you will find a lot of homophobia because of the way we all grew up.**
>
> *Billie Jean King*

THE OLYMPICS

The 2016 Olympics in Rio were groundbreaking for LGBTQ+ athletes, with a record 53 out athletes competing – Rio was called 'the gayest Olympics ever'.

Team GB's women's hockey team won gold for the first time ever in Rio. Teammates and wives Kate and Helen Richardson-Walsh are the first same-sex married couple to win gold medals in Olympic history. Flyweight boxer, Nicola Adams won her second gold medal for Team GB. Adams is openly bisexual and frequently features in polls of the most influential LGBTQ+ people in the UK.

Chris Mosier was a member of Team USA and the first ever out trans athlete in the Olympic Games. He is the founder of transathlete.com, a resource providing information on trans inclusion at all levels of sport.

SCHOOL

At school all students, teachers and staff should be respected equally regardless of their identity. It is particularly important for schools to be a safe space for LGBTQ+ students.

LGBTQ+ students and teachers have not always been able to rely on this safety. In 1988 the UK government passed a law known as **Section 28** which stated local government 'shall not intentionally promote homosexuality or publish material with the intention of promoting homosexuality' or 'promote the teaching of the acceptability of homosexuality as a pretended family relationship'. Organisations offering support to LGBTQ+ students were closed down. Section 28 was regarded as state-sanctioned homophobia by many, and it mobilised a huge number of activists to protest against it. The law was finally repealed in 2003. If Section 28 still existed, this book would not be allowed in schools.

Protestors display an anti-Section 28 banner at Pride, London, 1998.

BULLYING

Homophobic and transphobic bullying, intimidation and threats are harmful and hurtful. It can also lead to poor school attendance, underachievement, and serious physical and mental health issues for the abused person. For example, using the word 'gay' – to mean something bad – is homophobic and unacceptable.

"In the UK, 99 per cent of LGB students hear the phrases 'that's so gay' or 'you're so gay' in school."

Stonewall Teachers' Report, 2014

FROM PREJUDICE TO PROM

In the United States, under the **Title IX** law, schools are required to address any harassment against LGBTQ+ students or students who are perceived to be LGBTQ+. All students have the right to bring a same-sex date to the prom or school dance.

Gay-Straight Alliances (GSAs) are clubs in the USA that are open to students of any sexual orientation or gender identity. They can help make schools safer for everyone. If your school has extra curricular clubs, you have the right to start a GSA.

LGBTQ+ teachers – particularly those working in faith schools – can live in fear of losing their jobs just for being themselves. In the UK, LGBTQ+ teachers are protected by anti-discrimination employment law as enshrined in the Equality Act of 2010.

"In the USA 64 per cent of LGBT students feel unsafe at school because of their sexual orientation."
nobullying.com

"80 per cent of secondary school teachers in the UK have not received any specific training on how to tackle homophobic bullying."
Stonewall Teachers' Report, 2014

HARVEY MILK HIGH SCHOOL

Named after the gay rights champion and politician, **Harvey Milk High School** is an LGBTQ+ friendly public (state) school in New York City. Open to all students age 14+ regardless of identity and background, it provides safe learning away from the threatening environment many LGBTQ+ students face in mainstream schools.

Students arrive at the Harvey Milk High School on its opening day, 8 September 2003.

FAMILY

A family is typically a group of people related to one another. In the past, most societies expected families to consist of a man and a woman, and their children. However, the definition and understanding of family has changed and expanded.

Single-parent families, stepfamilies, families with more than one parent, extended families and many other family combinations have all contributed to changing our idea of what a traditional family looks like in the 21st century. LGBTQ+ activists have been instrumental in campaigning for the rights of all sorts of people to adopt children and build families, regardless of marital status and sexuality. Some families are built by parents adopting children, others through surrogacy – an arrangement whereby a woman agrees to carry a pregnancy for other people who will become the newborn child's parent after the birth.

BUILDING A FAMILY

In the past, laws prevented LGBTQ+ people from having custody of their children after a separation or divorce, and also prevented LGBTQ+ people from adopting, or receiving medical assistance to conceive. This made building a family very difficult for LGBTQ+ people. Now, many countries realise LGBTQ+ people have a right to family life and have removed barriers.

A family photo of actors Neil Patrick Harris (third right), his husband David Burtka and their two children. Harris and Burtka have chosen to be public about the fact that their children were born via surrogacy.

In 1996 Canada was the first nation to legalise LGBTQ adoption; now LGBTQ couples can adopt children in 25 countries around the world.

Since 2005 all LGBTQ people have had the right to adopt in the UK.

Adoption is a popular way for LGBTQ people to become parents. LGBTQ couples are four times more likely to adopt a child than heterosexual couples.

In the USA, adoption by LGBTQ parents has been legal in every state since 2015 and an estimated 20,000 same-sex couples are raising more than 30,000 adopted children.

TRANS

Transgender (trans for short) is a general term used to describe people whose gender is not the same as the sex they were born with, or does not feel like it matches the sex they were born with. Some trans people choose to change their bodies to reflect the way they feel inside, some may want to keep the body they were born with. Others might still be figuring it all out.

Some trans people struggle for a long time to be their true selves, and many around the world face transphobia and anti-trans laws which make it difficult or dangerous to be true to themselves. Some trans men and women come out when they are young, others may take a lifetime. No matter when it happens, it is a sign of bravery and strength to be true to one's self.

Transgender people are a part of all communities, ethnicities, ages and backgrounds and can have a variety of sexual identities.

CHANGES

For some trans people, changing the way they dress and present themselves is a first step in fulfilling their identity. Some trans people change their name, either informally or legally. This may be followed by surgery and taking hormones to adapt the body to its true gender. Not all trans people follow this route; some may opt for just surgery, or not take hormones at all. Some may keep their given name, adapt it, or ask to be called something completely different. The most important thing is that each trans person is able to choose their own path and be respected in their decision to do what is right for them.

The Transgender Pride flag combines the traditional colour for boys (blue) and girls (pink), with the white stripe representing an undefined gender.

TRANS PIONEERS

Surgery has been available since the 1920s, and the Danish artist **Lili Elbe** (1882–1931) was one of the first to undergo transitioning surgery. Elbe's life was the subject of the 2015 Oscar winning film *The Danish Girl*.

The first known trans person to undergo male to female transitioning surgery and hormone replacement was **Christine Jorgensen** (1926–1989). She was born in New York, and served in the US Army during the Second World War. In 1951 she travelled to Denmark to have a series of operations. When Jorgensen returned to America, she became well known following a series of newspaper articles she wrote. Jorgensen challenged the idea that gender was 'fixed' and could never change.

Lili Elbe

Christine Jorgensen

One of the earliest people to have male to female transitioning surgery in the UK was **April Ashley**. Born in Liverpool in 1935 as George Jamieson, Ashley had surgery in Morocco aged 25. She returned to the UK and worked as an actress and model, and was outed in 1961 by a tabloid newspaper. Ashley was finally legally recognised as a female after the Gender Recognition Act 2004 became law, and was issued with a new birth certificate. Ashley was appointed a Member of the Order of the British Empire (MBE) in 2012 for services to transgender equality.

April Ashley

Laurence Michael Dillon (1915–1962) is the first known female to male trans person. Born into an aristocratic family in Ireland and raised in England, Dillon started taking the male hormone testosterone in 1939 and later had transitioning surgery. Dillon managed to get a doctor's note in order to change his birth certificate, trained as a doctor, and published one of the first books about what we now call transsexuality. In 1958 when his birth sex was publicly revealed he fled to India and joined a Buddhist monastery. He died in India in 1962.

Laurence Michael Dillon

TRANS TIMELINE

1966
The **Beaumont Society** is founded in the UK, a national self-help organisation run by and for the transgender community.

1969
Trans women and other gender non-conforming people, including **Sylvia Rivera** and **Marsha P Johnson** play a crucial role in the Stonewall riots.

1972
Sweden becomes the first country in the world to allow citizens to change their sex.

1993
Brandon Teena is brutally murdered in Nebraska, USA.

1995
Mermaids, the UK charity for trans young people, is founded.

1998
Trans woman **Rita Hester** is murdered in Massachusetts, USA.

1999
On the first anniversary of Rita Hester's murder, on 20 November, an annual **Trans Day of Remembrance** is set up to recognise and remember all victims of transphobia and violence.

2003
National Center for Transgender Equality set up in the USA.

2004
Gender Recognition Act in the UK allows people to legally change gender.

2012
Equal employment opportunities and protection extended to all trans people in the USA.

2015
Caitlyn Jenner, formerly known as Bruce Jenner, who won an Olympic gold medal in the decathlon, is the first trans woman to feature on the cover of *Vanity Fair* magazine.

2016
Former US president Barack Obama issues a national directive permitting trans students to use school toilets that correspond with their gender identity.

Guardsman **Chloe Allan** becomes the first trans woman to serve on the front line in the British army.

Marsha P Johnson

Sylvia Rivera

Caitlyn Jenner

IDENTITIES

Identities of gender and sexuality were once believed to be set at birth. Now we recognise identities can change and evolve. The words we use to describe ourselves and others can be widely known and easily understood, or obscure and unique. It's important to respect sexual and gender identity even if we don't fully understand it. It's OK to ask questions in a clear and respectful way.

CHOOSING A TITLE

A title is used in formal situations, or when wanting to show respect. Mr, Mrs and Miss are commonly used. But there's also Mx. It is a gender neutral title used by non-binary people (see panel, right) and those not wishing to reveal their gender. It is used in Britain by the government and many businesses, and is gaining popularity around the world.

CHOOSING A PRONOUN

Not everyone uses the same pronouns to describe themselves. Many LGBTQ+ people choose different words to describe themselves. It's OK to ask people how they would like to be referred to. Some people prefer a gender neutral (sometimes called gender inclusive) pronoun, which does not associate a gender with the individual who is being discussed. This table shows how to use the gender neutral pronoun 'ze':

SUBJECTIVE	OBJECTIVE	POSSESSIVE	REFLEXIVE	EXAMPLE
SHE	HER	HERS	HERSELF	SHE IS SPEAKING. I LISTENED TO HER. THE BACKPACK IS HERS.
HE	HIM	HIS	HIMSELF	HE IS SPEAKING. I LISTENED TO HIM. THE BACKPACK IS HIS.
THEY	THEM	THEIRS	THEMSELF	THEY ARE SPEAKING. I LISTENED TO THEM. THE BACKPACK IS THEIRS.
ZE	HIR/ZIR	HIRS/ZIRS	HIRSELF/ ZIRSELF	ZE IS SPEAKING. I LISTENED TO HIR. THE BACKPACK IS ZIRS.

SEX AND GENDER

Sex is the term used to describe the biological and anatomical characteristics of an individual. The two dominant sexes are male and female, however there are many variations, including intersex – when a person has a mixed anatomy that is not clearly either male or female.

Gender identity is how we identify and feel about ourselves inside. It may or may not match the body we were born with. There is a wide spectrum of gender identities that extend beyond being a man or a woman. Even Facebook has 51 gender options to choose from! Here are just a few:

Non binary	not identifying as either male or female
Cisgender	having a gender identity that matches your sex assigned at birth
Genderqueer	an identity outside the traditional gender binary, with a political edge
Genderfluid	a mixed gender identity which can vary over time
Two spirit	a Native American whose body expresses both feminine and masculine spirits

EXPRESSING OURSELVES

Gender expression is how we show our gender to the outside world. There are endless ways to express our gender – whether as a boy who likes to wear skirts, a girl who likes to wear suits, a girl who wears dresses, a boy who wears trousers, or anything in between.

Not all people who wear the clothes or accessories of the opposite sex identify as transgender either. Cross-dressing has a long history, and may be done for performace, disguise, comfort or self-discovery. Drag is a popular form of cross-dressing performance, and, like everyone else, drag artists have a range of different sexualities and gender identities. It's never a good idea to judge people by what they wear, or assume things about them from their appearance.

A person's sexual identity is shaped by how they see themselves and the people they are sexually and romantically attracted to. This can be fixed or change throughout a person's life.

> " You can call me he. You can call me she. You can call me Regis and Kathy Lee; I don't care! Just as long as you call me. "
>
> *RuPaul, American actor, drag queen and singer*

LGBTQ+ AROUND THE WORLD

Rights for LGBTQ+ people in many countries have come a long way in recent years. But the world is a big place, and many LGBTQ+ communities around the world are still struggling for equality.

ARGENTINA

Nuestro Mundo ('Our World') was the first LGBTQ+ rights organisation in Argentina. Formed in 1969, the group fought to advance civil rights, but during the late 1970s many of its members were among the thousands who 'disappeared' (were murdered) by the ruling government. In the 1980s, the political situation changed and LGBTQ+ activists were able to speak out. Same-sex marriage has been legal here since 2010.

BRAZIL

Brazil has over 300 active LGBTQ+ organisations. The Brazilian Gay, Lesbian, Bisexual, Transvestite and Transsexual Association (Associação Brasileira de Gays, Lésbicas, Bissexuais, Travestis e Transexuais or ABGLT), was established in 1995 and is the largest LGBTQ+ network in Latin America.

The city of São Paulo holds the world's largest LGBTQ+ Pride celebration, with over four million people attending. Despite positive strides towards equality, Brazil is the most violent country in the world for transgender people; 546 murders of trans people were recorded between 2011 and 2015.

 JAMAICA

Anti-homosexual laws have been in place since 1864 when Jamaica was a British colony. All same-sex male sexual encounters are illegal, though female same-sex encounters are not explicitly outlawed. Violence against LGBTQ+ people is widespread. J-FLAG (Jamaican Forum for Lesbians, All-Sexuals and Gays) was founded in 1998 and was the first organisation in the country to promote LGBTQ+ human rights.

SOUTH KOREA

In 1993 South Korea's first LGBTQ+ rights organisation, Cho-dong-hweh was formed. The first Korean LGBTQ+ Human Rights Forum was held in 2008 and 'Rainbow Action', a coalition of LGBTQ+ organisations joined forces to fight discrimination. In 2013, transgender Koreans became able to legally change their gender, without having to have gender reassignment surgery.

INDIA

The cities of Delhi, Calcutta and Bangalore held their first gay Pride parades in 2008. In 2013 a campaign was launched to abolish Section 377 of the Indian Penal Code, a law against homosexuality, but the law was upheld and it is still illegal for men and women in India to have relationships with people of the same sex.

India, along with Nepal, Pakistan and Bangladesh legally recognises a third gender – *hijra* – an ancient transgender identity and expression.

AUSTRALIA

Australia inherited discriminatory laws from its time as a British colony. To challenge these laws, the Homosexual Law Reform Society formed in 1968 and achieved its goal of national decriminalisation 29 years later.

In 2004, LGBTQ+ rights activists established the campaign group Australian Marriage Equality, although same-sex marriage remains unlawful in Australia.

Chansey Paech, the first openly gay Aboriginal politician, was elected as a state representative in 2016.

ALGERIA

Homosexuality is completely illegal in Algeria, yet underground support groups and networks exist and even thrive. Alouen, meaning 'Colours', was founded in 2011 by a group of young volunteers with the aim to end LGBTQ+ discrimination and violence. The group holds an 'LGBTQ+ Day' annually on 10 October, calling for Algerians at home and abroad to light a candle in support of equal rights.

JAPAN

Homosexuality has been legal in Japan since 1880, but sexual orientation is not protected by civil rights laws which means that LGBTQ+ people in Japan are vulnerable to discrimination, and same-sex marriage is not legal.

In 2011 Japanese voters elected Taiga Ishikawa, the first openly gay candidate, to office in the city of Tokyo.

SAUDI ARABIA

Homosexuality is completely illegal in Saudi Arabia. Punishments can range from prison sentences lasting several months to life imprisonment, fines, whipping, chemical castration, torture or execution.

Positive media portrayals of LGBTQ+ rights is banned. Official LGBTQ+ organisations are not permitted to exist, and any gatherings must remain secret. In 2014, a 24-year-old unnamed Saudi Arabian man was sentenced to three years in prison and 450 lashes after he was caught using Twitter to arrange dates with other men.

ZAMBIA

Like several other African countries, Zambia inherited homophobic legal statutes from the British Empire during its time as a colony. Since independence in 1964, however, LGBTQ+ Zambians have faced repression, harassment, and open hostility from political figures. Many LGBTQ+ Zambians have to hide their identity, and some have been forced to leave the country and live abroad in countries where they can be more open.

CANADA

Same-sex sexual activity was decriminalised in 1969 and Canada now has some of the most inclusive and progressive LGBTQ+ rights in the world. LGBTQ+ Canadians are free to marry, adopt children and are protected by non-discrimination legislation.

POLAND

While homosexuality is not illegal in Poland, an official opinion poll in 2014 found that 70 per cent of Poles believe same-sex sexual activity is morally unacceptable. A giant rainbow made of artificial flowers, known as Tęcza or the 'Warsaw Rainbow', was installed in St Saviours Square in 2012 as a symbol of Polish LGBTQ+ equality; it has been repeatedly vandalised and restored.

GERMANY

Germany is regarded as one of the most LGBTQ+ friendly countries in the world. However, it was not until the 1980s that the LGBTQ+ victims of the Nazis were memorialised in cities like Frankfurt, Cologne and Berlin.

Karl Heinrich Ulrichs (1825–1895) was a German writer and pioneer of the modern gay rights movement. He wrote 12 books on the subject of same-sex love and spoke openly about his homosexuality.

LGBTQ+ LIBERATION TIMELINE

1895   Oscar Wilde is tried and convicted of 'gross indecency' and sentenced to two years hard labour.

1897   In Berlin, Magnus Hirschfeld founds the Scientific Humanitarian Committee – the first ever official organisation for homosexual rights.

1924   The Society for Human Rights – the first homosexual rights organisation in America – is founded in Chicago, USA.

         Panama, Paraguay and Peru legalise homosexuality.

1933   Denmark decriminalises homosexuality.

1934   Uruguay decriminalises homosexuality.

1937   A pink triangle is first used by Nazis to identify gay men imprisoned in concentration camps.

1940   Iceland decriminalises homosexuality.

1942   Switzerland decriminalises homosexuality.

1944   Sweden decriminalises homosexuality.

1950   Gay rights group the Mattachine Society is founded in Los Angeles, USA.

1951   Greece decriminalises homosexuality.

1954   Alan Turing commits suicide, after being forced to choose between prison or chemical castration as punishment for homosexuality.

1955   The Daughters of Bilitis founded by four lesbian couples in San Francisco, USA.

1957   The Wolfenden Report is published, recommending decriminalisation of homosexuality in the UK.

1958   The Homosexual Law Reform Society is formed, campaigning to end criminalisation of homosexuality in the UK.

1963   The Minorities Research Group is founded in the UK.

1966   The Beaumont Society is founded to promote trans rights in the UK.

1967   The Sexual Offences Act is passed, decriminalising homosexual acts between two men over 21 years of age in private in England and Wales.

1969   The Stonewall uprising and riots happen in Greenwich Village, New York City, USA.

1970   Foundation of the Gay Liberation Front in the UK.

1971   Nullity of Marriage Act passed, explicitly banning same-sex marriages between same-sex couples in England and Wales.

1972   Two thousand people gather for the first Pride in London.

1978   The iconic rainbow flag is designed by Gilbert Baker.

         Harvey Milk is assassinated.

1980   The first Black Gay and Lesbian Group is formed in the UK.

1982   Terry Higgins dies of AIDS and the Terrence Higgins Trust, the UK's first AIDS charity, is set up in his honour.

1984   Chris Smith speaks openly about his sexual orientation and becomes the first openly gay Member of Parliament in the UK.

1987   The International Foundation for Gender Education (IFGE) is founded to promote acceptance for transgender people.

AIDS Coalition to Unleash Power (ACT-UP) is founded in the US to highlight the growing AIDS crisis and demand access to medication for HIV-positive people.

1988   In the UK Prime Minister Margaret Thatcher introduces Section 28. Stonewall UK is formed in response to Section 28 and other barriers to equality.

1990   Reform Judaism, a branch of the Jewish faith, decides to allow openly gay and lesbian rabbis to serve communities.

1991   The red ribbon is first used as a symbol of the campaign against HIV/AIDS.

1992   The World Health Organisation declassifies same-sex attraction as a mental illness.

Press For Change, a key lobbying and legal support organisation for trans people in the UK, is formed.

1993   'Don't Ask, Don't Tell' legislation, limiting LGB acceptance in the US armed forces, is signed by President Clinton.

1994   UK age of consent for same-sex relations between men is lowered to 18.

1997   UK government recognises same-sex partners for immigration purposes.

1999   Trans Day of Remembrance is founded in the USA, and then later in the UK and worldwide, to remember those murdered as a result of transphobia and to bring attention to the violence endured by the trans community.

2000   The UK government lifts the ban on LGB people serving in the armed forces.

The age of consent for same-sex relations between men is reduced to 16, the same age as heterosexuals.

2002   Equal rights are granted to same-sex couples applying for adoption in the UK.

2003   Section 28 is repealed in England, Wales and Northern Ireland.

2004   The Civil Partnership Act is passed, granting civil partnership in the UK.

The Gender Recognition Act is passed giving trans people full legal recognition in their appropriate gender.

2005   Same-sex marriage is made legal in Canada.

2006   Same-sex marriage is made legal in South Africa.

2008   Proposition 8 is passed in California, banning same-sex marriage, just a few months after same-sex marriage had been approved by the state legislature.

2009   Iceland elects the first openly gay head of government in the world, Jóhanna Sigurðardóttir.

2010   Laws enabling same sex-marriage are passed in Portugal, Iceland, Argentina and Mexico City.

2011   Elio Di Rupo, first openly gay male head of government, becomes the prime minister of Belgium.

2013   Marriage (Same-Sex Couples) Act is passed in England and Wales.

Alan Turing is given a posthumous royal pardon for his conviction of 'gross indecency'.

2015   Same-sex marriage is made legal nationwide in the USA.

Ireland votes by a huge majority to legalise same-sex marriage, the first country in the world to do so by a referendum.

FURTHER INFORMATION

SUPPORT AND ADVICE

Avert is an organisation that provides information about HIV and AIDS but it also has a good general section which helps people to think more about gay and lesbian issues.
Web: **www.avert.org/teens.htm**

The **It Gets Better Project** has lots of videos showing people talking about the tough experiences they had as young LGBTQ+ people, such a being bullied at school, and that being LGBTQ+ does get easier.
Web: **www.itgetsbetter.org**

London Lesbian and Gay Switchboard provides free and confidential support and information to LGBTQ+ communities throughout the UK.
Telephone: **0300 330 0630 (daily 10 a.m.–11 p.m.)**

Mermaids provides information and support for people who want to know more about transgender issues.
Web: **www.mermaidsuk.org.uk**

Stonewall has support and advice on coming out as well as information on laws that affect LGBTQ+ people and information on how to take action against discrimination.
Web: **www.stonewall.org.uk/help-advice**

LGBT HISTORY MONTH

LGBT History Month is a month-long annual commemoration of lesbian, gay, bisexual and transgender history. In the USA it is celebrated in October, whereas in the UK it is celebrated in February. During the month many events are organised to increase the visibility and promote the welfare of LGBT people and honour the struggle for equal rights. This was started in the UK in 2005 by **Schools OUT UK**, who have information and resources for young people, parents and schools available on the following website:
//lgbthistorymonth.org.uk/

BOOKS

This Book is Gay by Juno Dawson (Hot Key Books, 2014)

Gay & Lesbian History for Kids by Jerome Pohlen (Chicago Review Press, 2015)

GLOSSARY

Age of consent The age at which a person is considered to be legally competent to consent to sexual acts. In the UK the age of consent is 16.

Amniotic fluid A clear liquid which surrounds and protects an unborn baby (foetus) while it is in the womb.

Bi or bisexual A person who has an emotional, romantic and/or sexual attraction to more than one gender.

Buggery A slang term for the act of sodomy.

Chemical castration A medical process where drugs are used to change the levels of hormones in the body in order to reduce the patient's sexual arousal or interest in sex.

Civil partnership A legally-recognised union of a same-sex couple, with rights which are similar to, or the same as, those of married heterosexual couples.

Closet/closeted A state in which a person will not talk about something, or tries to hide something.

Cold War The non-violent conflict between the USA and former USSR between the late 1940s and early 1990s. The era was marked by both sides building up large collections of nuclear weapons in order to threaten each other, but which they did not use.

Concentration camp A type of prison used during a conflict where people who are not soldiers are imprisoned under very harsh conditions. The Nazis used concentration camps during the Second World War to imprison people who they considered to be inferior (Jews, homosexuals, gypsies, political prisoners).

Cross-dressing The act of wearing clothes made for the opposite sex.

Drag king Performers (usually female) who dress in men's clothing and adopt exaggerated male gender roles as part of their performance.

Drag queen Performers (usually male) who dress in women's clothing and adopt exaggerated feminine gender roles as part of their performance.

Enigma machine Machines invented in Germany in the mid 20th century which created coded messages which were very difficult to decode. They were mostly used by the German armed forces in the Second World War.

Equality The state of being the same or equal, such as everyone having the same rights, freedoms or social status.

Gay A man who has an emotional, romantic and/or sexual attraction towards men. Gay is also a general term for lesbian and gay sexuality – some women prefer to define themselves as gay rather than lesbian.

Gross indecency A term used in British law since the 1880s to outlaw some sexual activity between men. The term was never defined in the law, meaning it could be used very widely to punish many types of activity.

Heteronormative An attitude or belief which promotes heterosexuality as the normal or better orientation or perspective.

Heterosexual A person who has an emotional, romantic and/or sexual attraction towards people of the opposite sex.

Homophobia The fear or dislike of a person or group of people who identify as being gay or lesbian.

Illegality Not allowed by law.

Intimacy A term describing emotional and/or physical closeness and warmth.

Lesbian A woman who has emotional, romantic and/or sexual attraction to women.

Nazis The political party (the National Socialist German Workers' Party) which controlled Germany from 1933 to 1945, under Adolf Hitler.

Oppression The act of treating a person or group of people in a cruel or unfair way.

Outing The act of revealing something about another person's identity, usually against their will.

Pansexual A person who has emotional, romantic and/or sexual attraction towards people regardless of their sex or gender identity.

Perspective A way of thinking about or understanding something from a particular point of view.

Posthumous A term which describes something happening to a person after their death, such as receiving an award or gaining recognition.

Renaissance The Renaissance was a period in European history between the 14th and 17th centuries, when there was a new interest in science, and in classical art and literature. We also use the term to refer to a period in time when there is a new interest in something that has not been popular for a long time.

Stereotype An unfair or untrue belief that some people may have about all people who share a particular characteristic, such as race, nationality, gender or sexual identity.

Subversive Secretly working to criticise, discredit or damage a system, such as a government or political system.

Suppression To force people to stop doing something or to keep something secret.

Transphobia The fear or dislike of a person or group of people who identify as being trans.

Transvestite A person who practices dressing and acting in a style or manner traditionally associated with the opposite sex. Some people find the term offensive and identify as cross-dressers.

INDEX